WITH GOD AND WITH MEN

ADRIENNE VON SPEYR

WITH GOD
AND WITH MEN

Prayers

Translated by Adrian Walker

IGNATIUS PRESS   SAN FRANCISCO

Title of German original:
Bei Gott und bei den Menschen: Gebete
© 1992 Johannes Verlag, Einsiedeln, Freiburg

Cover design by Roxanne Mei Lum

CONTENTS

CONTENTS

I

PRAYERS
OF THE EARTH

In the Morning

FATHER IN HEAVEN, you divided
day from night
so that both might become
a reminder and a joy for us:
a reminder to think of you,
a joy that we can serve you in any way.

So let this day that is just breaking
also belong to you.
Let it be a day of your Church,
a day of your children.

It is still entirely fresh, and it is as if
anything might yet be formed from it.
And we know that it is your property,
for you have created it,
and that in obedience to you we
should make of it a day of election,
a space wherein you could be at home
at any and every instant,
a space that is filled by you,
but in which you also demand of us
the service of the task that you assign us.

Let us be pure, give us the gift of a good disposition,
let us do cheerfully whatever our service requires.

You divided day from night,
but do not let us constantly divide
what we do with willing ease
from what appears toilsome to us.
Let us rather accept with joyful thanks
everything the day brings as coming from your hand,
let us enter into the spirit of it,
let us make of it what you intended.

Let us be clear of hearing as the day is clear,
transparent to you.
And if the day has turbid and unclear moments,
we shall know that
these are the unclarities of our unsure nature,
of our ignorance, which finds decision
hard.

You not only divided, from the very beginning
you decided:
let us also enter with decision into our task
and decide just as you expect us to.

You divided day from night for love,
let us live on your love,
let it take root in us,
let us bring together with your Son
every day's work before you
so that it may be performed out of your Spirit. *Amen.*

At the Beginning of Mass

LORD, WE HAVE COME TOGETHER in your house.
Let us recognize by more than outward signs
that we are in your dwelling place.

Let us, I pray, feel your Spirit,
so intensely that we kneel before you already
    transformed,
ready to receive everything you want to show us,
ready to leave behind everything
that is incompatible with you.

And just as we shut the door behind us
when we entered your sanctuary,
let us forget what belongs only to this world,
what tends to distract our thoughts from you,
everything that does not pertain to your love
and that is incapable of serving it.

For you see how weak and imperfect we are,
what an effort it was finally to make up our minds
to come to you today,
how much we make of every hindrance,
how eager we are to take other paths than yours.

So take away, Lord, our hard heart. Let us
nourish pure thoughts,
let us know deep in our spirit that we are in your
    house,

that we are awaiting you, that you have promised and
   given
not only your presence before us
but also your indwelling in us.

Bless this hour.
Yet bless it not only for us but for all
who spend it here with us.
For the priest who is celebrating,
for all priests who are celebrating Mass around the
   world today,
and for all those who are prevented from celebrating.

Bless it for all believers,
for the whole communion of saints.
Bless it, too, for all who are on their way to you,
who have not yet received the gift of faith,
for those who perhaps burn in expectation of
the moment when they may at last appear before you.

Bless it in our lands,
bless it in the missions,
bless it wherever men are,
and bless it so that they may bear fruit,
that, standing before you free from ourselves,
we may look upon no one but you.

That we may at last follow the path
that leads away from us toward you.
That during this hour we may not turn our minds
to all sorts of things that have nothing to do with you,
but may pray for what you point out to us;

with an open spirit, because you open your Spirit
    to us,
with a humble heart, because you wish to dwell
    in such hearts,
with a loving soul, because you are love itself.
Bless, open, grant us love. *Amen.*

Before the Sermon

W HEN YOU PREACHED on earth, Lord,
    you found the divine words
that were able to reach the hearts of your hearers.
Your truth moved them deeply
and prompted them to follow you and to live for
    you.

Lord, bless now the words of the preacher.
Allow him to forget himself,
his mediocrity, the effect he would like to
    produce,
so that he can speak solely and in all truth
of you and your doctrine.

So that he can say the things that all his listeners
    await,
something that truly comes from you,
laden with your love, filled with your wisdom,
which is not the wisdom of this world.

Grant, Lord, that the Holy Spirit may pervade him,
so that he may become a true mediator of your word.
But give to us, his hearers, a good spirit,
so that we may really hear your word
and not simply indulge our mania for criticism—
in our irritation at the mediocrity of what he has said
and at the faulty manner in which he expressed it—
to the point where we see only the preacher
and his weakness, and nothing more of your word
and Spirit.

Instead, let this hour become
a holy hour in which the mediator and the hearer are
united in your Spirit.

Help us to welcome your word
as the living word of God
and allow it to work in us,
so that we may take it home with us;
so that a bit of the Church may spring up
wherever we are;
so that our week may be filled with
the gift your grace gives us today.

Let us not forget what we have heard
but rather build on it;
give us the love it takes to build,
let this love work in us.

Remain the light of our days,
become the goal of our love,

and bestow on us through this homily
a new life in your faith,
a life that is both prayer and work
in your love. *Amen.*

After Communion

F ATHER, YOU HAVE GIVEN US the gift of your
living Son,
and you allow him to come to us again and again in
the Host.
You bestow him, not as just any life,
but as life of your life.

Let us welcome him in the fullness of his divine power,
which he possesses through his abandonment.
Let us yield to him,
so that he can work in us by the Holy Spirit.
So that, despite all our failings,
he may feel at home in us
and can go forth from our heart to carry out
your will in us;
so that we may do nothing to frustrate or diminish
his work in us.

Do not permit us to measure everything in our
limited way,

to take precautions and to feel worries that have
    nothing to do with him.
Let us, as far as we are able,
emulate and follow him.

There are so many whom you grant today
the grace of receiving him;
allow each one of them to take along all the others
who are hindered from coming, who are not
    admitted,
or who do not yet know your Son as they do.

We thank you, Father, that you let your Son become
    man,
that you allowed him to make the sacrifice of the
    Cross
and also granted him the sacrifice of the altar.
We thank you for every grace
that each one of us receives
through him.

But leave our thirst for these graces,
permit us always to yearn for them;
not only for ourselves but for all those
for whom your Son died on the Cross
and who, by the power of the triune God,
will rise again with him and through him.

Father, bless every communion, make the meaning of
    the Eucharist
come ever more alive in your Church.

And do not let this vital sense be bound to the limits
of our knowing and willing,
but let it pour itself out unhindered
from its source: eternal life.

In our thanksgiving we are united with all those
who know you
and who are permitted to receive the benefits
of your Son's mission.
And with all those who endeavor to consecrate
their lives to you as a proof of their thanks.

Grant us the strength to give these thanks a form
in which you can recognize your Son's hand at work
and can perceive
in the spirit of our thanks your Holy Spirit
and can use us for whatever you will.

Give us a willingness that comes from your Son's
willingness,
let us become loving by sharing in the love with which
he achieved his mission,
the mission to love you in perfect obedience
and thereby to redeem us for you. *Amen.*

Evening Prayer

ALL WHO BELIEVE in you, Lord, see
how night is falling;
their daily work is through,
grant them rest. A rest
that comes from you, that accompanies them,
that relieves them of the burden of the day,
of its cares and its anxiety,
and leaves them wholly refreshed.

Give them wholesome thoughts and fruitful prayer.
Let them feel you nearby.
Let them learn of your kindness.
Let them fall asleep thinking of you.
And when they wake again,
may they know that you were at their side
and that you will order everything again for the
    coming day
and will not abandon them but will come to their aid.

You can do this: you can give them new strength,
give them a new outlook on things,
allow them to begin again.

Be with those who sleep and with those
who cannot sleep.
And if they cannot sleep
because they are racked by worry,
ease their anxiety.

And if they cannot sleep
because they are in pain,
show them the meaning
that you yourself put inside suffering,
so that, through the pains
they must now undergo,
they may feel your presence.

Give them profitable thoughts
that can follow them even in
the severest torments.
Welcome graciously whoever dies this night,
bring him to the Father as your brother,
efface his sins from your memory,
grant him a new life that lasts for ever.

And be with your Church.
Be inside all those darkened churches
that are empty of men during the night,
the churches in which you alone keep vigil
with your small sanctuary lamp.
Fill the whole space with your presence
so that those who enter tomorrow morning
may receive the gift of a new strength in prayer.

Be with your whole Church, who is your bride,
let her live as a bride,
never led astray by any temptation.
Grant her above all the gift of that love
which united you with your Mother,
the love by which the Mother

became a bride for you,
just as today your entire holy Church
is destined to become your bride.

Sanctify the whole creation of your Father;
live in everything your Father has created
as a sign that his work is good,
as confirmation of the reality of the redemption.

And let the Holy Spirit blow through the world
so that it might be converted
and that you might bring back to the Father
his redeemed creation in its fulfillment. *Amen.*

Before the Tabernacle

L ORD, I WOULD LIKE to thank you
for your presence, for seeing
in this house the house of your Father
and for dwelling in it;
you did not want to be far from us and hidden
with the Father and the Holy Spirit,
but to continue to abide in our midst
as the way that leads to the Father.
As the way by which we also
come into possession of the Holy Spirit.

I would like to thank you for being here,
concealed in the mystery of the Host,

yet so very present that it is you yourself who
    teach us
to pray and who help us to live.
So very present that we come in order to receive
    and to take
the gifts your presence brings us:
the assurance of faith,
the love of your dwelling among us.

Lord, you know how weak we are and how far
    we have turned away,
you know that we consider everything else more
    important than you;
yet you keep leading us back to this place
where you abide in order to change us.

Lord, let your Holy Spirit
take possession of us once and for all,
so that on all our ways we may know that
you are walking with us,
that you help and answer us.
For you do not make us worship you
like some distant sovereign
but are a brother who loves us
and who accompanies us constantly.

Let us live for this love
that unites you with the Father in the Holy Spirit.
Let us perceive it, at least sense its presence
    everywhere,
so that we may no longer hinder its working

but may be pervious to your grace;
so penetrable that with your help
we may live in your service
and collaborate in your work.
In this way we will lead to you more who love you,
in order to multiply in the world that love which
    desires
to encounter you, the Father, and the Spirit.

Your presence here is the presence
of your love for us, it is wholly an act of love,
which also embraces every state, every disposition
of love.

When you became man and
dwelt among us as a child,
your Mother was at your side.
She lavished on you the purest love,
but even this love was a gift of your
presence, a gift that you made her.

It was a mother's love that smoothed your way,
that served you, that had no other interest than
caring for you,
while adoring the Father in the Son.
You formed this maternal love
to be an example for us too.
Teach us to look at your Mother,
let us draw our love for you from hers,
let us adore you with her

and together with her be well pleasing to you
in the same service of love. *Amen*.

Prayer to the Risen Lord

L ORD, WE THANK YOU for the Easter feast.
We thank you that after your death and
your descent into hell,
after tasting to the full every kind of abandonment,
you have returned to us;
that you have remembered our insignificant
   abandonment
and overwhelmed it with the radiant fullness of your
   presence.

Although you suffered the death
that we caused
by the burden of our sins,
you come back to us as our brother
with the gift of your redemption.
You do not make us pay for
having brought you to the Cross
but let us take part in your joy.
You celebrate a reunion with us
as if we had never been unfaithful,
as if we had always awaited you
with faithful trust,

as if we were capable of adding something
ourselves to your joy.

Lord, make us grateful.
Let the thanks we owe you and
your Mother
always accompany us from now on,
let them bear fruit,
let them be the pervasive spirit of our service.

Let us be redeemed men who truly fill
their whole life with your redemption,
follow you wherever you go,
and attempt to do your will,
just as you do the Father's will.

Do not let us merely enjoy the fruit of your Passion
and of your redemption;
let us try, starting today,
to know you as our brother, as our true redeemer
    ever in our midst,
and always to bear in mind that you are present
and that you have repaid our unfaithfulness with
    fidelity
and our unbelief with even greater grace.

Let every day, whether hard or easy,
dawn as a day
that holds the express, or even hidden, joy
of knowing that you have redeemed us
and, returning to the Father, have taken us back
    with you.

We ask you now for your Easter blessing;
may it include the blessing of the Father
   and of the Spirit. *Amen.*

Prayer for Renewal of the Spirit

D EAR LORD, you see how we get used to
   everything.
It was with joy that we once took up your service,
firmly resolved to be totally dedicated to you.
But because every day brings nearly the same thing
   over and over again,
it seems that our prayer has contracted.

We limit it to ourselves and to
what we deem necessary
for the task we have to perform right now,
so that in the end our prayer has been reduced to
the dimensions of this small chore.

We beseech you now, do not permit us
to become so narrow.
Give us new breadth, give us once more something
   of the elastic
vigor of Mary's Yes,
which is ready for the entire divine will,
which always remains as wide as it was when it was
   first pronounced,

and which is ratified anew every day.
Whether Mary rejoiced or was afraid or hoped,
whether she was tired from her daily round of duties
or was being led to the Cross:
she always stood before you as if for the first time,
was always obedient to whatever you said,
always hoped to be allowed to do all that you wished,
always saw behind every one of your wishes, even the
    most insignificant,
the great, unlimited will of the Father,
which you, her Son, were fulfilling.

Grant that we may contemplate and affirm you and
    your Church,
and carry out the requirements of our mission
in an ever new spirit,
the spirit of the Mother's Yes.
Grant also that we may pray for this spirit.
We know that wherever you send your Spirit,
you yourself are present.
The Spirit brought you to your Mother,
the Spirit enabled her
to carry you, to give birth to you, to surround you
    with care.
And because you recognized your own Spirit
in her,
you formed your Church from her.

And since you have called us into this Church:
make of every one of us a place

where the Spirit of your Church blows,
where, together with you and with the help of
the Holy Spirit,
the will of your Father, of our Father,
is done, so that we may dare to pray in earnest:
"You, our Father, who art in heaven. . . ." *Amen.*

Prayer for Indifference

LORD, YOU KNOW that I would like to serve you
but that I am still attached to my work
and to my judgment;
that I am constantly
scurrying back into myself to
survey everything from my angle of vision:
that I do *this* in order not to do *that*,
that I desire *this* and loathe *that*.

Whereas you showed us in every moment of
your earthly life, and especially on the Cross,
what it means to do the will of another.
For you this other was the Father,
the Father who is so perfect that
you regarded every one of his decisions as
perfect and accepted it in advance, without
sizing it up first yourself.

Not because of any judgment you might have
  arrived at
after trying and weighing each case,
but out of love.
Your love for the Father took the place
of your personal scrutiny once and for all.

And you have also given the gift of this love
to your saints;
and your saint Ignatius has spoken
and has written about it
and has shown how the will of the superior,
the will of the Father,
the divine will pure and simple,
is the decisive motive
for the one who loves,
for the one who no longer cares for anything but
  the wish
of the beloved.

Grant us a share in this power of your Sonship,
allow us to learn to love the Father
in the way that you love him,
to come to him through you and your filial attitude,
to become obedient
by the strength of your perfect obedience,
to become indifferent by your indifference.

Grant that we may no longer seek our own interests
  in anything,
but that, together with your saint Ignatius,

our interest may go immediately to you,
and we ourselves may become indifferent to the very
    core of our heart;
not in order to lose all interest in you and the world,
but in order to begin, at long last, to love
you and the Father in the Holy Spirit
above all things. *Amen.*

Thanksgiving after Confessing at the End of the Year

L ORD, WE THANK YOU for the gift of confession,
     for having taken away all our sins
by your death.

When you did this, you showed us how total
nakedness before the Father,
how standing ready before him, doing his will,
remaining where he has placed us
all belong to the essence of true confession.

And now, as we come to the end of this year,
we are conscious of having often done wrong.
We have neglected so many things that, in keeping
    with your will,
we ought to have attacked with gusto.

We have not paid enough attention to your voice,
we have not truly lived for you alone.

For we should have sought you
in all things,
we should have relished the year's joys
as coming from you,
we ought to have taken on ourselves its sufferings
as willed or permitted by you,
we ought to have followed every path
you opened to us.

And yet there is no need
to look back dolefully on this year,
for like every year it was a year of your grace.
A year in which you helped us,
ceaselessly encouraged us,
and showered us with joys and
an endless number of good gifts.

And if we have not discovered you in all things
and have failed so often to meet your expectations,
today your grace permits us
to have the refuse cleared away from us.
You cleanse, you mend,
you make all things new in us
and together with us.
And you do all this by the power of your Cross.

You suffered this Cross on Good Friday,
and, in spite of our denial,

you made so many feasts of redemption come after it
on the strength of your Resurrection.
And the absolution you give us
is a perfect one:
you give us the gift of a new purity,
in union with the Father in your common
Holy Spirit, in the eternal purity of the Trinity.

And so we do not have to keep building
on an imperfect and unstable basis
but have the grace of a new beginning on the
    foundation
of your own perfection, which you communicate
    to us.
We have the grace to join in your work of
    construction,
to walk, to hope, to labor at your side.

This is how confession shines into our daily life,
this is the effect of absolution.
It irradiates and causes that joy
which sprang first from your Cross
and throughout all the days of the past year
was enough to show us plainly your task.

Therefore, we thank you for having done everything
    for us
exactly as we needed,
we thank the Father, who let you become man for
    our sake,
we thank the Holy Spirit,

whose constant effort has been
to realize your mission in our existence.
Amen.

The following prayers were written for a sick nun:

Prayer in
Passing Time

F ATHER, YOU HAVE ENTRUSTED to us this
passing time
as a gift of your grace
and presence.
As you live in eternal time, so we—as long as we
live—
must exist in transitory time.
Not abandoned by you, but in a connection with you
that you prepared and provided from creation
and that has gained new density and strength
through the coming of your Son.

And if the years vanish in their course,
they are still only successions of days
that pass right through us
as we pass through them
in order to seek constantly what you have to show us,
to experience constantly your love in new ways,

to remain constantly in your embrace,
just as the whole of time
remains in the embrace of eternity.

We know that we are in your hand,
that you shape all things,
that you demand of us only
the attempt to love you as steadfastly as we can.
Not you in isolation, but
you with your Son and
your Spirit in the unity
you manifest from the primordial beginning of
    eternity.

Our love can only be
response and requital,
because you, triune, eternal Love,
always love us first;
but do not permit this answer
to wane in us;
rather, let it be so vigorous
that you can always perceive in it the reflected
    brilliance
of your light. *Amen.*

Through Mary to Christ

I

Through you, Mother, we have come
   to your Son.
You conceived him, you carried him,
you gave birth to him,
you accompanied him throughout his life,
in order to bring him to us and to give him to us.

And also in order to show us how a man
can bear and understand him,
how a man can place his life within
the life of your Son,
so as to receive it from him.

In order to convey to us
the gift of his infancy, of his years at home with
   you,
the gift of his public life
and of the hour of his Passion.
At every phase of his life you were so involved
that everything his presence conveyed
found room in your receptive heart.
Yet not for you, but for us.

By your Yes, you placed yourself so totally
at the disposal of the Father, the Son, and the Spirit,
that the triune God gave us to the Son
right through you.

You led us to him, but you were always so much
   in God,
so much within your mission
and your own Yes,
that your only desire
was to act as the conveyor of the gift
and not as the original giver.

Yet for that very reason your act of conveying
also became a gift
that came from your humility
and that your humility gave us.
A gift to us,
but also a gift to God.

And we would like to ask you today
to accept into your Yes all
that makes up our lives, not just its joys,
but also its sacrifices, the roads we take
that we had not reckoned on before.
Do this so that we may once again come to your
   Son through you.
So that through you, who knew so well
how to carry out the Son's will,
we, too, may now accept anew everything
he intends for us in the will of the Father,
may now will it anew because it is his will.
But also that through you we may will anew,
with you, grateful that everything you did
occurred entirely within his mission.

And when the sacrifice costs more than we
    thought,
when it is harder to bear than we imagined,
we want to remember that you did not shrink
    in fear from any sacrifice,
and that you did everything in the joy of
    your Yes.
And we want to ask you to intercede
for us with the Father, with your Son, and
    with the Spirit,
so that we may be permitted to live
by your strength,
to come in reality to the Son through you,
and to do in him what *you* have done for him
all along.

And when you see your angel, Mother,
remember
that his appearance assured
you of the way.
Ask him to surround us
with care out of love for you, just as he did
    for you,
to intercede for us just as he interceded
    for you
and, by his appearing, gave you the power
to say Yes in faith to everything.

II

Lord, before you became man and
entered into your Passion,
you invited your Mother
to serve you as mother,
to bear your sacrifice with you,
but also to share with you your joys.

And the grace with which you endowed her
and by which she became your Mother
is so inexhaustibly great
that there is room in it for all who seek you,
for all who in their faith desire
to offer you sacrifices.
The sacrifice of a life in your service,
perhaps even the sacrifice of giving up this
    service,
or the sacrifice of
unforeseen humiliations and sufferings.

And because you so loved your Mother
and granted her such a pure love for you,
we ask you, Lord, to receive us, too, every day
into this grace,
to show us a place in your relationship
to your Mother,
a place that allows us to offer up anew
each one of her sacrifices, to experience together
    with you
each one of her joys, and to do forever precisely

what the Mother, with you, and
with the Father and the Spirit and all the citizens
    of heaven,
expect of us.
Grant us the joy and the grace of serving
today and in eternity. *Amen.*

Prayer for the
Right Use of Illness

LORD, BLESS THE SICK. All who know
or feel that they are sick,
all who are in pain,
all who are about to die.

Bless them not merely with enough strength to
    endure the pain,
bless them also so that they may learn
to bear it for you and
to see in suffering a grace.
Show them that every suffering has been
given a meaning by your suffering on the Cross,
a meaning that the Father has integrated
into the meaning of your own suffering
and has made useful for the redemption of the world.

Show them that, if they are willing
to suffer in your name,

pain and illness become fruitful;
that you can use them to help others,
to lighten *their* load,
to unblock paths
that would otherwise be closed.

Give them not only strength and courage but also
    patience.
Give them, lastly, love for the sufferings
that are asked of them:
the love that can spring only from your love
and can bear fruit only together with your love—
even though this fruit is hidden from their sight,
even though they do not know where you
intend to use the grace that comes
from their suffering.

May your grace enable them to radiate such love
in the midst of their illness
that others are infected by it,
that their suffering helps
to transfigure the suffering of others,
that it reveals to the nurses and doctors who work
    with them
a reality that until now they had not known,
that it becomes a fresh revelation to their visitors
of the meaning of life and death.

Give them all such a state of maturity
that they may accept absolutely everything
as coming from your hand

and see in every pain
something that surpasses all pain:
your grace. *Amen.*

Prayer for
Times of Weariness

D EAR GOD, I am too weary
to pray.
And you learned on the Cross
how great weariness can be.

I beg you,
let all your angels
and all your saints so adore you
that nothing is missing from adoration.
Amen.

Prayer of an Old Nun

D EAR GOD, you know that I became
a nun in order to serve you
and that my decision
was not exactly easy.

You gave me confidence back then;
I knew that you had
chosen this way for me yourself.

And you have given me from day to day
my whole life long new courage
to try to offer you everything.

But you know how it goes in a life
that is supposed to be consecrated to you:
both the small and the relatively big sacrifices
recur in a sort of regular rhythm,
so that one gets a little used to them.

And now you are asking for a really big sacrifice:
I am supposed to put back in your hands my life as
    a nun
just as you gave it to me.
I cannot walk any longer,
I cannot work,
I cannot choose myself what to offer to you
    throughout the day.
Sacrifice has now taken on a different form:
I must simply accept everything
and can only offer you again and again
the prayer that all may be done according to your
    will.

Show me, I ask you, how to do this,
so that you may be pleased,
so that you can recognize
in me your own service,
so that it is no longer I, but you in me,
who perform it, you with your Mother
and with all the saints.

This doing will thus become fruitful
and partake of the fruitfulness
of every hour of your life.

I pray you, do not let me
grow weary, even in my weariness, of offering up
everything to you.
And bless this suffering, for your whole Church
and for all who seek the way to you. *Amen.*

Prayer at the Approach of Death

LORD, BECAUSE WE TAKE your death so lightly
that we rarely even think about it,
the thought of our own death is also
strange and distant.
Even when stern messengers forewarn us,
we manage to stifle the thought of our death
and to go on living as if our earthly existence
would never end.

And yet one day we realize
that we have to die;
grant, Lord, that we will not be wholly unprepared.
Let us understand our death in relation
to your death:
let us know that you died for us all

and that when we die we
have no choice but to be with you.

You have transformed the punishment of our death
into the grace of the eternal life to come.
You permit us to rejoice in this gift of yours.
Even when the passage proves difficult,
even when the pains become overpowering,
while the anguish increases and uncertainty
masters us,
let all this agony happen
if you will it so,
so that you may get something from our life,
a late fruit
that is at last at your disposal.

Let us die just as you will,
whether in fear
or in absolute pain
or in sleep
or perceiving death approach hour by hour.
But however it may turn out, let us not
abandon the thought of you
but rather know that every death, even death in
    darkness,
is your property
and has already been experienced in you on the Cross.

Let us die as believers
whose faith also shines upon the others
who assist at our death,

brings them help now, and perhaps later,
when their own hour comes, gives them consolation.

Lord, make known your presence
to all who survive us;
help them to weather their grief,
be with them to the end of their days. *Amen*.

The "Suscipe" of Saint Ignatius

TAKE, LORD, RECEIVE

TAKE MY WHOLE LIFE, take it, I pray you, just as it is now, with everything that goes into it, with my powers, my desires and efforts, but also with everything in me that still tends away from you, everything I have laid in reserve for myself; take all of this, along with everything else, which I now offer you. Take everything and make it entirely yours.

MY ENTIRE LIBERTY

The freedom of my days, the freedom of my thoughts, the freedom of my work, even the freedom of my prayer. Make out of all this freedom a pure service of your freedom; dispose freely of my freedom, see in it nothing beyond my wish to serve you. This is the choice I now make: to commit my entire freedom to you.

MY MEMORY, MY UNDERSTANDING,
AND MY ENTIRE WILL

Take my memory, so that it may no longer be filled up with things that belong to me but may be cleared out and made ready for you again, ready to hold only what you store in it. Take it as you would take an object that until now has served a particular end but that has just been freed up for any sort of employment you have in mind for it. And take my understanding, which clung to so many things and tried to grasp so many things that were not of you. May it become an understanding of your service, which is at your disposal, so that it takes in only what you want to enrich it with and what can be of service to you. Therefore, let everything it contains that is incompatible with you and your intentions sink into oblivion. Take also my will, which was so often just self-will, which over and over again distanced itself from you. Take it away from me at last and fashion from it a particle, as it were, of your will, which is always filled with doing the Father's will.

YOU HAVE GIVEN ME ALL
THAT I HAVE AND POSSESS

Lord, you have given me the things I need in order to live—daily nourishment, life with all its small, often unnecessary comforts. You have also given me time out of your own store of time, the days to work and the nights to rest. You have given me thoughts, prayer, and, finally, everything I myself am and have and become. All this is your gift, and I have no right to anything. I have earned none of it for myself and have received nothing from anyone but you.

TO YOU I RETURN IT ALL

Not by scorning it and casting it away, for I would like to offer it to you just as I received it, as little damaged as possible, with no other meaning and value than those you intended when you gave it to me. I would also like to offer it to you in as living a way as I received it from you.

I COMMIT IT TO YOU
FOR YOUR ENTIRE DISPOSITION

Let it be so completely entrusted to you that you can utilize it without regard for the giver, like anything you please, which you are free to use or not; I pray you, consider it your property, just as I, alas, considered it my property as long as it was in my hands. I would like to leave it in your hands without counting the cost and without ulterior motives and from now on see in all reality, in things and days and nights, nothing but your property, which is yours to do with as you please and which by that very fact alone acquires new meaning.

GIVE ME ONLY YOUR LOVE AND YOUR GRACE

Your love was always the love of the triune God, in which you allowed us to participate and which we have idly spurned by sinning. Give me this love now on the condition that I deem it the highest good and do not prove myself unworthy of it time and again. I need it more urgently than the air I breathe; therefore, let it be such an urgent imperative for me that it becomes a spur prodding me to serve you better. Let it be offered to you along with everything else; let me treasure it as you yourself love the Father whom you obey.

THEN I AM RICH ENOUGH

Rich and enabled to serve you, for your love contains everything needed by one who believes and hopes. Thanks to this love I am as rich as you yourself in your return to the Father after the accomplishment of your mission. As rich as the Father when he welcomed you back, as rich as the Spirit when he reunited you two, because your triune love is so infinite that there is room in it for everything and is enriching only as a creature can be filled to overflowing with goods when it lives by the love and grace of God. For faith can wish for nothing with greater longing than to take part in eternal love, and love can eternally love only itself in its triune fulfillment.

Prayer That Saint Ignatius
Taught Adrienne

CORPUS CHRISTI, adoro te tribus sub tuis formis,
  sub forma divina, simili deo patri,
sub forma hominis, sacrificii et crucis,
sub forma hostiæ rotundæ, sine principio et fine.

Ubi es, est amor sempiternus,
omnia tangens quæ creavit pater,
omnia quæ passus est filius,
omnia quæ vivificat spiritus.

Amorem tui cum gratia mihi dones, ac dives sum
satis nec quidquam ultra posco. *Amen.*

———————

Body of Christ, I adore you under your
    three forms,
under the form of God, in which you are equal to the
    Father,
under the form of man, of sacrifice and of the Cross,
in the form of the Host, which is round without
    beginning or end.

Wherever you are is the eternal love
that touches all
that the Father created, all that the Son
suffered, all that the Spirit vivifies.

Give me your love and your grace, then I am
rich enough and wish for nothing further. *Amen.*

Prayer for Constancy

LORD OUR GOD, give your children ready
perseverance in loving you.
You know all too well what we are like:
moved by your goodness when it comes to us
   unexpectedly,
dismayed by your severity
when it reveals itself to us with its demands.

When we live through happy or hard days,
we think of you, seeing what comes from you;
but in the monotony of every day we grow lukewarm,
we forget you,
we keep you far from our thoughts
and from our action,
as if we needed you only on the
eventful days,
as if we wanted to have you at our disposal.

We beg you, change this, let us turn back
while there is time,
act decisively, tear out our tepidity,
replace it with fire or cold
or with both at once,
only, allow your Spirit to blow in us.

Destroy everything that is not yours, and let us
think no thought whose center is not you,
so that by this destruction
we are compelled to a livelier love.

We do not demand of this love that
it be painful or delightful,
only that it be yours, forevermore.

Lord, give us the grace to offer you again and again
what you have given us.
Only in this way will we unprofitable servants not
remain fruitless.

Bless your love in us,
so that it may yield the fruits
that you desire. *Amen.*

Prayer for Those
Who Have Turned Away

W E CAN UNDERSTAND death and sickness
and even poverty, Lord;
but how can anyone turn away from you
after having known your grace?
That is an unfathomable mystery to us.

After all, it would be quite easy for you
to make the signs of your grace so obvious
that no one could have any more doubts about
    them
or to bring back those who are leaving

with a gentle call: and you do not do it,
in your wisdom, you do not do it.

Lord, allow us just the same to beg you
with our whole soul
that our cry might pierce through the
    lukewarmness
of those who are drawing back;
let our members suffer for them,
accept every sacrifice for them, only,
we implore you,
enable them to return, make it easy for them,
and in exchange let us pay the price
that you deem just.
We will try to give you
what you take,
but grant them anew your faith,
your grace.

And at the same time we know
that we ourselves take our faith too lightly
and are given over and over again to promises
that seem hard
when it comes time to keep them.

Lord, grant us all your mercy
and strengthen our weakness. *Amen.*

Prayer for
Liberation from Oneself

LORD, SET ME FREE and take me to yourself.
You have shown me the chains that hold me back
from my way,
and if they still exist to hinder me,
it is for no other reason than that in my heart of
hearts
I am not yet willing to detach myself from them.

How often I moan and groan and regret
having so little freedom,
whereas all I really mean are
the obligations that daily life
and my profession entail;
but these obligations do not really
block my path,
they do not affect its essential course,
at most its outer form;
if anything, they are perhaps
just little tests.

What weighs so heavily does not come from outside;
it lives and takes shape in my own self—
I mean everything to which I am attached,
which I am not disposed to renounce,
which serves me as a crutch and a convenience,
everything to which I believe I have a right.

Take, Lord—I am trying
to ask you for this sincerely—
everything that in my eyes
is part of my rightful spiritual property,
but that paralyzes my love for you,
that makes your love for my neighbor
stop flowing and freeze solid.

Let me disappear
in the flow of your love to all men,
so that it can pour itself out unhindered. *Amen.*

Prayer for Usability

FATHER, LET OUR WHOLE LIFE become a prayer
that rises up to you like fire and
sweeps along in its flame
everything evil and impure,
all that belongs to us and to others,
so that you may fill it up with your Spirit
and may make it good enough to become yours
and to be used by you.

Do not leave the evil in us either, Lord,
but turn it back;
open us to your action,
even when it is painful;
allow our conversion,
allow it in your own name. *Amen.*

In the Passion

Lord, in your Passion your glory
disappears more and more;
as the Son of man, you become
pure man, so infinitely like us
in your misery and nakedness.

And if we contemplate these things—
whenever you grant us to behold them in truth—
we remain before them as if out of time,
and what we experience is terrifying in its duration,
but even more terrifying because of its content.
All that we are enters this state
of being only man,
which is solitude, yes, abandonment.

You suffered for us immersed so deeply in the night
that we no longer even know
that there is a Resurrection.

Lord, the burden of our sins
on your shoulders is becoming unbearable to us.
Design the way, give it the form
you wish,
the form of a cross, if need be. *Amen.*

To Surrender What
We Do Not Possess

LORD, SO OFTEN I have given you
what I possessed in abundance;
let me now offer you everything
that I do not have,
that has always been denied me,
that I have sought half-suspecting
it was unattainable:
peace, rest, shelter.

And if I know now that all this belongs to you,
that it remains in your safekeeping
and is your possession,
I will no longer clamor for it.
The constant, vain running of my restlessness
no longer troubles me:
rest is in you, you have taken possession of it,
even from me;
you can dispense it again without loss;
in you is shelter—
who else would have it?—
you can deal out this gift.

Be praised: what we seek is found in you,
and what we fancied we were giving you generously
was in you from the beginning.
And yet we thank you that in spite of this
you accept it from us as well.

Lord, do not just take what we do not have:
keep it.

Planting is the Lord's alone,
to us he might leave the gathering of a few ears
of his sprouting seed;
that which was already his
is what we bring before him.

A living fire does not cease to burn
until all is consumed and reduced to ash;
no one regards the ash;
strewn lifeless on the ground,
it cannot fructify, hidden as it is,
but it can be trampled completely into the earth,
serving a task of which it knows nothing.

Lord, burn us to ash,
and scatter us according to your will.
If I should ever say again what I will,
do not grant that prayer:
believe, even against every appearance,
that from now on I am yours alone
and know no other will than yours. *Amen.*

II

PRAYERS OF HEAVEN

It would be more precise to characterize these prayers as prayers of the Church on earth as they sound in heaven before God's throne. For the Church, on earth and in heaven, is just one Church. As the earthly Church, she is instructed about the heavenly Church by means of the Apocalypse.

"God's Glory Illuminated Her and Her Lamp Was the Lamb"

LORD OF OMNIPOTENCE and lord of impotence,
you reveal both at once in your holiness:
your omnipotence, which can overcome
and direct each one of us,
and your impotence, which has to wait upon the love
  and surrender
of each one of us.

Whenever someone is ready to take the way
that you yourself are and that
you prepare for him,
you place at his disposition your entire holiness
as the light in which he can walk.

Without this light that you provide, there would
  be no portal for him to find and
no way before him.

Without your light, none of those who believe in
    you would attain
even a slight degree of holiness.

For our holiness is the meeting
of your light with the faith in us—
the faith we have always received
from your light in the first place.
And you allow us
to reflect its beams together with you.

In the midst of the city, you have set up the sign
    of your Son's Cross as the sign of the highest
    holiness.
And when you let your people walk the way
of holiness, you give them,
in the mode and manner
that pleases you, this Cross for the journey,
so that they may accept it,
bear it, and bring it back to you,
the almighty God, in your Son's company.

You allow your Son, accompanied by your saints,
to give back the Cross he bore,
but you also receive it jointly with the Son,
so that he may see that you, Father,
recognize in every one of your servants
the countenance and the work of your Son.

You have given these servants the gift of holiness
that your Son won for them on the Cross.
In order that he may learn in perfect love for you

that you have accepted his perfect offer,
you allow the imprint of the Cross to be seen in the
   sacrifice
your saints only attempt to offer you.

All of us who have received from John
the message of the perfect city
want to serve you with renewed love,
with renewed faith and renewed hope.
We all want to use all our
failing strength to help
in the realization of your Son's work,
so that his glorification of you, Father,
may be manifested also in us and in all who are
   entrusted to us
in your whole Church. *Amen.*

> *"The Walls of the City*
> *Had Twelve Foundation Stones,*
> *on Which Were Written*
> *the Twelve Names of the*
> *Twelve Apostles of the Lamb"*

It is supposed to become apparent how the Apostles' Creed opens the twelve gates. It is not as though one article each of the Creed were attributable to an individual apostle or held particular meaning for him. Rather, the spirit of the grace of the apostles, who all share their missions with one another

—inasmuch as all of these missions flow from one source, the Lord—opens all twelve gates of the city. At the same time, all twelve articles are proclaimed not only by all of the apostles in common but also by each one in his own particular way. In this prayer it is revealed how the Apostles' Creed looks in the light of the heavenly city; how the Creed can become prayer in the spirit of heaven.

I. I BELIEVE IN GOD,
THE FATHER ALMIGHTY,
CREATOR OF HEAVEN AND EARTH

GOD, HOLY FATHER, you created heaven and earth and have filled them now in John's vision with a new light. You have shown him your creation, how it appears when the light of your holy city illuminates it, and this light with which you fill the city is you yourself. Your light has shone through all things, the entire city has become translucent, luminous, glistening, and fruitful in the holiness with which you have invested it. We pray you: Give the gift of this same holiness to your whole people, to your Church, to your priests, to all your faithful, to all who seek you, to all who aspire to truth as well as to those who already possess it; for it is the light of your love.

2. AND IN JESUS CHRIST,
HIS ONLY SON, OUR LORD

God, Father, you have given us your only Son: he is our Lord. You have bestowed upon us the gift of faith in him, so that our gaze may pass right through him to see you as you yourself deign to be revealed to us. We all pray you: Accept graciously our memory, our mind, our will, so that everything in us may be filled by this faith born of your light. We all pray you: Give us the light that you grant us through faith in your Son, so that we may transmit its radiance— just as you also first gave it to your Son and he transmitted the gift. Let our faith in your Son become the kind of faith that your perfect light requires.

3. WHO WAS CONCEIVED BY THE HOLY SPIRIT,
BORN OF THE VIRGIN MARY,
WAS CRUCIFIED, DIED, AND WAS BURIED

Father, you have given us your eternal Son in such wise that his life among us can be recounted with words that can also be used to describe and sum up a normal human life. But at the beginning, you sent him forth and let him be carried into the Virgin's womb by the working of the Holy Spirit; and she carries him now and will give birth to him, just as you eternally generate him and carry him in your bosom. And by his birth from the Virgin Mary, you have permitted all of us to share in the mystery of this birth in the Spirit and have allowed us to participate by faith in your Son's own growth in obedience and wisdom. We pray you, grant that the life of those who belong to you, the life of those who believe in you, may be summed up as plainly and simply as the earthly life of your Son. Let every life to which you have given something of your own holiness become what it was meant to be, so that it may be worthy of the grace your Son offers it. Let the Holy Spirit take an active part in our generation and growth. Allow your Son in accordance with your will to give us for your glorification a life that may count as a life of one of his brothers in you, Father.

4. HE DESCENDED INTO HELL

Your Son, Father, let himself be sent beyond his death on the Cross into hell, into that most abandoned, most desolate region in which no living man has ever set foot. He did this in order to share better in all your mysteries, in order to show you that he is never complacent in your service, in his love for you. He offered you the "extra" by going even farther with his descent into hell. Father, since we know what your Son suffered and endured for our sake out of love for you, let us prove ourselves grateful for it. Moved by the same love that you give to your Son in the Holy Spirit, let us attempt to offer to you and to him everything we do and suffer, hope for and love, in a manner pleasing to you. Do not let the grace of your Son be wasted on us. Let our answering Yes resound with such ringing finality that you can accept it as an irrevocably valid word. You can really hear it as such, because the overflowing love and grace of your Son that are bestowed upon us guarantee that his own powerlessness to go on will be inserted where our feeble powers fail, in order thereby to round out our mere attempt to an actual accomplishment, indeed, to his accomplishment, which he presents to you, to your eternal light, through his descent into darkness.

5. ON THE THIRD DAY HE ROSE AGAIN FROM THE DEAD

Triune God, Father, Son, and Spirit, let the Son's rising again from the dead into eternal life signify a renewal of every single believer, the renewal of the Church as a whole, and, through the Church, the renewal of the entire creation. Let us, feeble as we are, be so bolstered by the might of his Resurrection that its grace may bring to pass our renunciation of that old life that up until now we called our own. The Lord has visited the dead and has risen from their midst, so that all the dead—the dead who are already buried and the dead still dwelling on earth —might obtain a share in his Resurrection. By rising he brought his work on the Cross to its ultimate fulfillment. Permit, Lord, that we may allow ourselves to be drawn up with you, that we may venture to emerge with you from our graves, even though this increases the burden you have to haul up from below. Do not let any of us see corruption and decay, take us all with you to God. Give us a share in the light of your Resurrection, a light that shines again in the light of your heavenly temple, that you accord to the holy city together with the Father and the Spirit.

6. HE ASCENDED INTO HEAVEN
AND IS SEATED AT THE RIGHT HAND
OF THE FATHER

Father, you have once again received at your side your Son, who, with your holy consent, distanced himself from you to become man. And you have given him, him alone, the place of honor at your right. He is enthroned next to you. You are enthroned with him in the joy of perfect heavenly reunion in the unity of the Holy Spirit. We pray you: Let your Church partake of this joy. May she never leave her place in this uniting of your Son with you. Father, allow your Son to bring your whole Church along with him, just as she believes in this union on earth today, and just as it is seen and praised in the holy city in heaven. Look not, O Lord, upon our infinite distance, upon all the defects and flaws that burden us; rather, receive us by the grace of your holy Church in heaven, by the power of the grace of all the saints who intercede for us; receive us, so that we may rejoice in your countenance and may behold you and your Son enthroned at your side in the unity of the Holy Spirit.

7. HE WILL COME TO JUDGE
THE LIVING AND THE DEAD

Father, you favored us in your Apocalypse with a glimpse into your judgment. You showed us the glory of the holy city only after we had experienced for ourselves a taste of judgment. And, Father, your Son wrote down something in favor of each one of us in his book of life. And this was an expression of his love. Grant your approval, so that this love may be the truth; and grant that each of us may be admitted to your presence. Give us this grace, bestow upon us this light. After your judgment has purified us and your fire has burned to ash everything in us that separates us from you, allow that this judgment of your Son's love may deem us acceptable and bring us to you—even though we stand before your judgment as great sinners and only at this moment realize the abysmal depth of our offenses. Let this be done for the love you bear him, in your own name and in the name of the Son and of the Holy Spirit.

8. I BELIEVE IN THE HOLY SPIRIT

Father, I believe in the Holy Spirit because you have given him as a gift through the Son; because you promised him to us already in the Old Covenant; because you give him anew to every believer in holy baptism and confirmation. I believe in this Spirit because you sent him to your twelve apostles after your Son had returned to you. When you sent down the Spirit on Pentecost, you gave us new hope in him. The grace you granted us by the coming of the Son from heaven, by his dying and rising, is not concluded with his Ascension. You allowed your Son to send down the Spirit from above; in this way you demonstrate to us that the Son received such a welcome when he returned to you after accomplishing his mission that the graces will not cease descending from heaven to earth. And so you gave us unending hope. Father, leave us this hope so that it becomes ever-new faith and remains ready to be strengthened ever anew in the light of your holiness. Give us above all the love of your Spirit, in your name and in the name of the Son and in the name of the Spirit of this love.

9. IN [THE] ONE, HOLY, CATHOLIC CHURCH

Lord, you have bequeathed us your holy Catholic Church as your bride, who is charged with telling us about you, her bridegroom, and with making him take on life in us. You declare yourself to be the bridegroom of this Church before the Father and the Holy Spirit in the communion of your Mother and all the saints. With all of them you are present to us and for us in the Church, which you raised as an indivisible unity of love to rescue the world on the verge of perishing. So we thank you, Lord, for the gift of your Church; let the expression of this thanks be our faith. Recognize by our faith, though weak and tepid, our gratitude to you and to the Father and to the Spirit for having given us in the Church the promise to take us up into the common light of your triune love.

10. THE COMMUNION OF SAINTS

Father, you have shown us the Bride of the Lamb, the holy city in heaven. We were permitted to see her so that we would wish to learn more and more of you and to be struck more deeply by your light. You have shown her to us in her perfect spotlessness and holiness, as she receives your light without the slightest cloudy dimness. We know, Father, that we are sinners and are quite far from having received as much holiness as is needed to be admitted to your holy city. But, Father, you have given us an image of this city in your Church, and you allow us by the faith you give us to enter into communion with those who are in truth saints and so, by the power of your faith, to take part even now in the holiness of heaven. You also incorporate into your Church every one of us who is willing to believe in order to make him a partaker in the bride of the holiness of your Son. We thank you for this gift; it is a gift that grows as you dwell ever more deeply in us. Grant, Father, that each of us may be admitted into this communion of love and that each of us may show many others the way into this communion. Allow this communion to multiply by your grace until it reaches the full number your Son merited for her on the Cross.

11. THE FORGIVENESS OF SINS

Lord, we stand before you as sinners. If we looked merely at ourselves alone, our confession would never end. Wherever our eyes rested, we would recognize our sin, which we have committed in intention, word, and deed. Not only individual sins, but their endlessly linking chain. Lord, you mounted the Cross for these sins, you suffered, died, and descended into hell in order to pay for the forgiveness of all our sins. And you have offered us the chance to tell forth our sins in holy confession, in humility and contrition, but also in the certainty of your forgiveness. You forgive us in judgment so that we may enter into your presence in heaven. Everything you show us of this heaven, of the life of the Trinity, of the city of your saints, has thus become for us a future reality. It is a reality in heaven, but we will come to share in it by the forgiveness of sins. And you show us the way to break away from our sins: we are to keep our gaze on you more than on our sins, to hope more from your grace than to fear from our sins. For your forgiveness is more than a mere erasure of our guilt; it has its full dimensions in the vision of you, in the love you give us to pass on to our brothers. Where sin once was, there is not a yawning void but your shining countenance: may we communicate this radiance beyond ourselves to all around us.

12. IN THE RESURRECTION OF THE FLESH AND THE LIFE EVERLASTING

Lord, just as you rose from the dead and appeared alive once more, dwelling among your own, you allow us also to rise again in our flesh. We are permitted to rise again as who we are on earth, endowed with the gifts with which the Father invested us at the creation, but purified now by your grace, filled with your gift of the communal Holy Spirit, who proceeds from you and from the Father. We are permitted to rise again, not for a brief moment that would be commensurate with our earthly life, but for an endless eternal life—your life, which knows no limit—which for us will be a participation in your fulfillment, in the eternal love between the Father and you in the Holy Spirit. *Amen.*

The Book of Life
of the Lamb

LORD, YOU CAME into the world
as the eternal lamb of the Father
in order to bring life to all.
Not only your limited human life,
but your eternal life.
In obedience to the Father, you
brought your whole life into the world for us,
you communicated it to us, to every one of us.

And you fulfilled the longing
of whoever of us bore in his heart
a yearning for life
by filling it to overflowing
with your own life.
You spent your life with such lavish prodigality
so that every one of us
could gain life in abundance,
and this superabundance is a promise
of eternal life.

And so that no one may be overlooked,
so that you can show the Father
that you came in order to redeem each one
and to lay down your life for each,
you have recorded in your book of life every one
  of your redeemed.

This book has thus become the sign for the Father
that you have not forgotten anyone,
that you desired to take everyone home.
Not only did you save our life while on earth, on
the Cross,
you have furnished proof of this salvation in
heaven as well.

Lord, teach us to be thankful for this.
Teach us to consecrate our temporal existence to you.
May it be spent in your service,
let it show you
that we have at least some inkling of
the greatness of your sacrifice, of the value of your
gift,
of the excess of your prodigal generosity.
For your gift to us is nothing less
than eternal life.

Teach us to embody your life,
so that even our earthly life attests:
we bear eternal life in us.

We pray you, therefore:
do not consider it a sacrifice,
when we dare to try this,
accept it merely as a token of our love,
since this love originates from you and from the unity
in which you live with the Father and the Holy Spirit.
Amen.

Thanksgiving for
the Apocalypse

FATHER, YOU HAVE LET Saint John glimpse
into the fullness of your glory.
What you showed him of heaven
was a part of your splendor.
You have shown him this
so that in his turn he might show it to all of us.
As an encouragement, as a help, as a sign that
the promise of eternal life is fulfilled.

You have allowed him to see the beginning of this
   fulfillment.
For what he was permitted to see
was not a remote promise
but its immediate fulfillment.
You have made him this gift for all of us,
so that we might all be granted a grander, more
   Christian,
more ecclesial conception of your grace
and your love.

You have granted him admittance into your heaven,
allowed him to see your angels
and the entire communion of the heavenly city.
Afterward, when he came back to earth,
into the solitude of his Christian life,
he knew that you were not leaving him alone in his
   solitude,

that you had not forsaken him in his abandonment,
and that solitude and abandonment and
temptation exist only in order to smooth the way
into your heaven for those who belong to you;
in order to give them the chance to shoulder a part
of the burden your Son bore in this life for all
with the intention of bringing us with him;
in order to give every one of your faithful
an understanding of just what it means to help your
    Son bear the burden.

But it has also become easier now in this solitude and
abandonment to share and to accept the burden,
    because you have
revealed to Saint John the end and the beginning
of this sharing.

And it ought to have been clear to us, Father,
that whatever you have shown us
of heaven always corresponded to the love
that binds you in unity with your Son
and the Spirit;
that your heaven with its visibility,
your eternity with its promises,
are only signs of your eternal love
into which you have determined to introduce us.

And in all the angels and in those
who accompanied John, you have shown
that while we are still on earth you give us heavenly
    companions

whose task is to help us
to find more easily the gates of your heavenly city.

In the name of your love we thank you
for your love. *Amen.*

Prayer of Adoration of the Servants before the Throne of God and of the Lamb

L ORD, WE PRAY YOU, fill our entire prayer
with your own word.
Let your word be conceived in us
in such a way that, when we pronounce it, it can
be acceptable to your hearing.

Do not let this word leave us behind;
grant that it may take us where it goes,
in conformity with your will
to have us in your presence.

Grant, Lord, that by your strength and
your holiness we may learn to glorify the Father, you,
and the Spirit just as you expect us to do.

Not only that: let everything in us that is not yours
   perish,
annihilate it so utterly that it can never return.
Let it disappear so completely that you can no longer
   see in us,

in any one of us who believe, anything but what is
    yours.
Your own, which you bestow upon us as a gift and
    which increases
in us by your grace alone.

Grant that by the force of the word that lives in us
we may live only for your service.
That the whole of everything we do or want or strive
    for
may pertain exclusively to your service.

Give us a share in your adoration of the Father,
do not grow weary of strengthening our weakness—
even though you do this by setting your weakness
in the place of ours—
so that we may help you to carry on
your task of glorifying the Father.

Make us this gift out of the treasury of strength
that your saints lend us.
Draw this gift from the promised strength
of the full realization of heaven. Give us this gift
remembering all that you suffered for us.

Grant that we may remain true and that every breath
we take may be filled by your Spirit.
For then we would be just as we ought to be
according to your intention,
as you saw us in the will of the Father
when you left heaven to save us.

We ask you for this because your Mother
has already asked you for it,
and because she showed by her life, by her
    accompaniment
during your earthly existence,
how serious she was about her offer
and how seriously we could mean it
if, supported by her purity
and thankful to her for bringing you to us,
we dared at least to try to go her way with her
in your strength.

Let your Mother supply what is
still lacking in our prayer,
let her adoration of you move you
to give us the gift of the spirit of this adoration.
We ask you this in her name,
and we ask you also in the name of the Father,
in your own name,
and in the name of the Holy Spirit. *Amen.*

"God the Lord Is Their Light"

FATHER, YOU ARE ETERNALLY in possession
of the eternal life
that you are now revealing to us from heaven.

You show it to us so that we may bring our
knowledge of it into our everyday life of faith:

it is permitted to accompany our earthly life.
Not, however, as if it made our present existence
appear valueless and no longer worth living,
but because you allow
us even now to give away the life we live today,
to place it at your disposal,
as a sign of thanks for the eternity
you grant us.

We know that this is how you conceived
our earthly life, which you gave us
to spend entirely in purity and grace.

We turned away, and you sent
your Son to us so that by his Passion
he might transform our turning away from you
    back into
a turning toward you.

And in doing this, he showed us by his life
that a human life is not something worthless.
And if he did not need it himself,
in order to prepare himself for eternal life,
all the more did he make of it
a preparation for us.

Your Son, Father, had eternal life in himself
when he shared our life.
He had it in himself to such a degree
that, through the grace of his sojourn among us,
we attained the certainty that we, too,
are permitted to carry this eternal life within us.

We pray you, Father, allow even our everyday
   existence
to become an answer to your eternity.
Give us the strength to bear the weight of your
   eternity
already now;
we do feel that it is a burden,
because we are not yet so fully purified by you
that we can consider it a pure gift.

Our life on earth still has an expiatory side;
but we want to be grateful to you
that your gifts are often heavy to bear.
And yet they are so full of grace,
so filled by your presence
that we joyfully say Yes
to all that you give us; knowing
that—in fulfillment of your promises—
we can bring what you give us into eternal life,
just as in heaven it will be definitively yours,
together with your Son and
your Holy Spirit.

Let us, Father, come to you,
but on the path you choose according to your will;
give us only the love that your eternity
pours so generously into each day. *Amen.*

Our Father

OUR FATHER

FATHER OF YOUR SON and Father of all who believe in you and who by the grace of the Son and of the Spirit come to you, Father of creation, Father of the Old Covenant, Father of the New Covenant, Father of each one of us.

WHO ART IN HEAVEN[1]

You are in heaven, you are the light of heaven. You are the light of every holiness, the light of faith, the light of hope, the light of love. You are in heaven, where in your triune spirit faith, love, and hope are found in the unity of light, in that unity which constitutes heaven, your heaven.

HALLOWED BE THY NAME

We want to keep your name holy by the holiness you have shown us in your light.[2] We want to re-

---

These notes ought to be taken into consideration above all because, dictated in response to questions posed afterward, they show how laden with meaning the individual words, which may appear flat to us, were for Adrienne.

[1] A parallel between the triune God and the trinity of faith, love, and hope, which *become* a unity, just as Father, Son, and Spirit *are* unity. Faith, hope, and love are in God, but God forms out of them his dwelling, his heaven.

[2] This is the perfect holiness that is made comprehensible to us by

main aware, to remind ourselves daily forever more and without interruption that your name contains every holiness.[3] We want to bow down before this holiness, we want to guard it as the secret that binds you together intimately with the Son and the Holy Spirit and includes us all when we look upon your light.

THY KINGDOM COME [TO US]

In the name of that holiness of yours that we have beheld, let, we pray you, the kingdom of your light come to us, let it shine in our darkness, let it make days out of our nights; let the grace of your kingdom arise where just a moment ago there was the bitterness of our sin. Receive our earthly life into your eternal life, as a token that you will to make our earth pass into your heaven in the new form it receives there.[4]

God's light and in his light. If God had not shown it to us in his light, we would have been constrained to form our own picture of it, and it would have appeared to us infinitely diminished. But since it has been shown in God's light, we have a real knowledge of the divine holiness. Even when the light is afterward darkened again in us, we know what this holiness essentially contains, inasmuch as we have seen it in God's light.

[3] In other terms: the word of the Son reflects for us the light of God's holiness. On earth we have the holiness we see in heaven in his word, and now we see God's holiness in both at the same time.

[4] In the measure that God allows our life to participate in eternal life through faith, he allows his kingdom to have come in us.

THY WILL BE DONE ON EARTH
AS IT IS IN HEAVEN

Father, together with the Son and the Spirit you have a single, divine, holy, indivisible will. Let it be realized in us, just as it has been realized in your heaven of light. Allow us to fulfill it, just as your Son has shown us that it is to be fulfilled.[5]

GIVE US THIS DAY OUR DAILY BREAD

Give us for every day the bread we need in order to be able to serve you. Give us the bread for our body, so that it may fulfill on earth its entrusted task within your will, so that it may prepare itself already while on earth for its life in heaven after the resurrection of the flesh, that it may become an instrument that enables every one of your servants to carry out your service as long as you need him here below.[6]

---

[5] It is the will of the Father that has been fulfilled in a visible, comprehensible way by the Incarnation. This will ceased to be something abstract for man from the time that the Son realized it day by day and shaped every day on earth into a vessel of the Father's will. In the act of his coming and in his remaining within his mission, he shows us how this will is to be fulfilled; the Son himself is in the act and the state of fulfilling.

[6] The daily bread has its unity in the service of God: it is bread for service. Bread of the body, as explained in the prayer; bread of the spirit, as doctrine, prayer, contemplation; these three as well in the unity of service, so that the spirit may learn to serve, may become fit for service.

AND FORGIVE US OUR DEBTS

Father, forgive us our debts, show us each time we have fallen that your Son died for each one of us; at each confession let us experience anew that after our confession we are once again received into the grace of your obedience—of the Son's obedience to you. Forgive us all our debt, for no one less than your Son died, out of love for you, for every single one of our sins, forgive us our sins out of the love that unites you with your Son.[7]

AS WE FORGIVE OUR DEBTORS

We ourselves want to learn to forgive; you show us how to do it by forgiving us, who are guilty of no less than the death of the Lord. Your forgiveness was so great on the Cross that it—with the impotence that was all your Son had left—has taught us to forgive in faith.[8]

---

[7] Forgiveness of sins and obedience belong most closely together. Obedience in the sense of utmost obedience on the Cross and at the same time as our obedience in confession: this is what has the power to forgive sins.

[8] We *are* forgiven, by grace and gratis. And so we receive in this forgiveness a surplus energy of forgiveness, which must be lavished on those who owe us some debt. This energy comes constantly from the Son, who constantly takes our sins upon himself. By forgiving us and showing us what we must do, it is almost as if he already forgives in our place those whom we have to forgive.

AND LEAD US NOT INTO TEMPTATION

For we are weak, Father who art in heaven, we know how weak we are, how easily we stumble; our blundering begins every moment we forget you and cease to fulfill your will in the measure that you expect of us. Lead us not into temptation, for you see how weak our entire pledge remains, even when it is given with the force of our faith. Accept it, in spite of that, as a firm promise, because you know that, in virtue of your Son's grace, his whole love is also contained in it. But do not, when you lead us into temptation, allow us to frustrate this love of your Son. Do not test our weakness so far that it would no longer correspond at all to the forbearance of your Son with us and to the love he poured out into us.[9]

BUT DELIVER US FROM EVIL

Deliver us from everything that is impure, unholy, from everything that would be ours and that would evade your light. Shine through us completely, let us become transparent, let us in the light of your Son's Cross become worthy of the light that, together with

---

[9] We are weak because we are sinful. Yet there exists a parallel between our weakness, which is one of sinfulness, and the impotence of the Son, which is a weakness of purity. If the Father does not lead us into temptation, it is because he remembers how weak purity made the Son on the Cross.

the Spirit, you bestow upon the saints. Let it be so,
Father, in your name, in the name of your Son, in
the name of your Spirit, and in the name of all your
saints. *Amen.*

"I Am the First and the Last"

LORD, YOU TELL US from heaven
that you are the first and the last.
Make us understand in faith this word
that you address to us again and again,
that you speak again and again like a declaration
    of love
to us and to the Father at the same time.

Let us understand the significance of your word,
become the first in our day
and remain he who is both first and last at once
until our evening.
Hold the place of the first and of the last
in every one of our thoughts, so that everything
we think,
embraced within your presence,
may become a prayer.

When you give yourself this name,
you offer yourself to us

as our beginning and end.
You offer to perform all
the work in us, to bring us
to the Father worthy of your promises.

Lord: mold us, mold our faith,
mold our life out of your own primacy as
beginning and end.
Uproot everything from us that does not
begin and end in you,
everything that prevents us from following you
    perfectly.
When you are the beginning and end in us,
your obedience to the Father comes to life
    in us.

Lord, let our obedience be offered to your
    will,
give us each day new strength to receive you
as our first and our last;
as the Father possesses you in the Spirit as
his first and last Son,
so permit us to learn from your Father,
from you, from your Spirit,
to possess our beginning and our end
forever more in you. *Amen.*

"He Who Hears,
Let Him Say: 'Come!'"

AT THE ORIGIN of all things, O Lord,
God the Father summoned you:
"Come!", and you came.

This summons, which you heard
and which you answered,
you also place in us,
so that it may possess in us the living force
truly to summon you.

You allow even us
to summon you: "Come!"
And by allowing us this, you show us
that you will to answer the summons
and to come,
that you are even now coming,
that we need only call you,
that we are permitted to expect you.

You hear. You hand over to us this summons
with the whole force of your divine will:
you place yourself completely at the disposition
of this summons that you suggest to us.
As if you were the servant
and we the ones in command.
In this "Come!", you give away

to us your secret. The secret that you never hear
    a question
without answering it.
You allow us, in whatever state we may be in, to call
    for you,
and you come.

Lord, grant that each of us, grant that your whole
    Church,
grant that all who have not yet found the way
to you and to your Church
may learn—each one separately and all together,
particularly all in your Church—
to let your summons ring out.

Teach us to say: "Come!"
In the same spirit of prayer
that you poured into our hearts
when in our midst you began to pray:

Father, thy kingdom come! *Amen.*

III

MARIAN PRAYERS

Prayer of Mary
Expecting the Child

She has given her Yes and knows that she will not take it back. She adores the Father, she adores the Spirit, she adores the Son.

FATHER, YOU HAVE GIVEN ME your Son.
He comes to me as God
and as the baby I am expecting.
Father, your handmaid is unworthy.

I spoke that first Yes in faith,
in confidence, in hope.
In the knowledge that your will for me had to be
    done.

I spoke this Yes in the Spirit of your Son
who is becoming my son.
I could not leave him without an answer.
For through you it was my baby who was asking me.

Father, now I am greatly afraid.
It is the fear of your mystery,
the fear of not being adequate to the task
you are setting me.
How am I, your handmaid, supposed to raise
    your Son?
How am I supposed to accompany him in his early
    years?

How am I supposed to teach him
to speak to you?
How will he learn from me
to adore you?

Father, I ask you for one thing:
keep my Yes,
keep it even now that fear is filling me,
keep it always as the word
that I myself do not have the strength to pronounce
but which in spite of that I have given to
my baby.

God the Holy Spirit, I have said Yes to you too.
I have said Yes in order to become a mother,
the mother I am expected to be for my baby.
The child has been entrusted to me
because he has already destined me
long ago to be his mother.

And now a great fear of this mystery
is filling me.
I know that I have given you not only my
body but also my spirit,
so that you might impregnate both,
in such a way that both truly serve the Father's Son
whom you have brought me.

But I am afraid. And I do not know
whether your Spirit takes away the fear in my spirit
or instills it in me.
All I ask is that you keep my Yes,

that you give me the strength to keep showing you
   every day
that I really intend to say Yes.
That is why I am asking you for your own Spirit,
which belongs to the Father and to my Son.

My child, my God, I adore you.
You are still too small to understand
my fear,
and yet, you are my God.
You are the God whom we have awaited for so long
and who has chosen me
to be your mother.

And even though I am so frightened now,
I am not worried about you, for I know
that you will know fear such as no one ever has
   before.
And I do not ask you to take
this fear from me, I ask you only
to make it fruitful in you
and, when you experience
the abyss of human fear,
when the Father and the Spirit abandon you,
to remember in spite of it all that you have a mother
who knows your fear,
a part of it at least.

Grant, Father, Son, and Spirit,
that by your grace I may fulfill my task, which I myself
   cannot understand,

according to your expectations.
And dispose of me day by day
according to your good pleasure,
always hearing the Yes,
even if I no longer should have
the strength to pronounce it. *Amen.*

Mary's Prayer in the Family

The Mother has grown accustomed to her baby, she loves and fondles him, she lives in a motherly and womanly relationship with him as if the child were an ordinary human child and the family a normal human family. And suddenly she realizes that he is the King, that he is God; that her love for the child is legitimate but at the same time is in need of an infinite expansion; indeed, this has already been initiated and yet must be lived anew every day.

FATHER, I HAVE SO OFTEN SEEN in your child
only my child
and in my love for him have again and again proved
my mother's love,
which was the child's due.
And my service of him was any mother's
service of her child.
I accepted everything
as it presented itself naturally,

I kept pace with the child step by step
and almost forgot that he was your child,
my God, who is destined to be the King of the
  universe.

And you want to open my love so wide
that the entire suffering of your Son
can find room in it. As much suffering
as a child can cause his mother,
as much suffering as the human God
can share with a believer along the way,
as much foreboding of suffering as a human heart
  can take
as an effective way of helping to bear the coming
  suffering of the Son.
The Cross that is meant specially for Christ the King
and will make him a truly divine King in the world.

With you, Lord, love is so close to pain,
and until now it was often
as if my love left pain behind.
But now you are stretching this love out
to encompass endless pain,
the pain your Son has in store for me,
because he must fulfill among us his task,
which is your mission.

And I know, Father, that
my task is comprised in his.
He has planned it in advance,
and it is he who fulfills my task.

It is always simply to say Yes,
a Yes of fear, a Yes of suffering,
a Yes that becomes inaudible and yet is heard.

Father, please, accept this Yes
that I pronounce only haltingly
as your Son pronounces it.
He says it with his divine confidence,
and I repeat it after him, in weakness and fear.
But just as he has taken up my task into his,
he has also drawn my Yes into his Yes;
hear, I beseech, his Yes
when you hear mine.

And I have no desire to count the days
and hours of my joy
but to lay everything in your hands
according to your need at the moment.
Give me everything in this way and not
    otherwise,
so that your Son may also receive
from his Mother the help in suffering he
    needs,
even if this help will serve
to make of him the King of sorrows,
who nonetheless in his kingly glory
reflects your glory.

I pray you, Father, in your name,
in the name of the Spirit,
and in the name of our Son. *Amen.*

Mary was, humanly speaking, surprised again and again at the fortunes that were reserved for her Son and her. Nevertheless, she had in God an anticipatory insight into the direction of her Son's path. She was aware of his expiatory mission and knew that this mission had to find its ultimate expression in death. She did not know the times, but she did realize where the way was leading.

Mary's Prayer in the Adult Years of the Lord

The Son is embarked on the active life. She remembers that, during the thirty years he lived with her, she knew ever more clearly that he is God and King. And she prays to the Father, to the Son, and to the Holy Spirit at the same time; and she associates all three most closely in speaking to them.

G OD, YOU ARE LOVE,
and in love my Son
came to earth
in order to be King of us all.
And you, Father, have shown me again and again
  in the Spirit
and in your Son
that he is coming into his kingship.

Not King in the sense that
unbelievers understand it,

but King in your sense, Father.
A King who brings ready with himself his
kingdom, your heaven,
and a King who possesses everything
and keeps nothing for himself;
who distributes the whole of his property—
the truth of heaven—
and gives it wholly to each.

And every beneficiary of this gift
receives the kingdom and the truth,
and in every one of these kingdoms
you recognize your own kingdom,
brought to us by your Son.

So long as my Son stayed with me,
I had a notion of his kingship.
I saw him pray.
And I saw how every time he prayed
your heaven stood open
and your kingdom was coming.

Now he has gone forth as King
to bring your kingdom to all.
He has set out,
taking nothing with him
but this truth
that was at home with us
and now knows no homecoming,
so that he may become more and more
the perfect King.

His kingdom is completely invisible
and is the perfect truth,
and it is given away both invisibly
and visibly.
This visibility becomes evident to faith.

And he roams from one place to another
like a beggar,
because he is a King of the eternal truth,
and the whole kingdom wanders with him.
And because the whole kingdom accompanies him,
he can take unknown roads
away from all of us into foreign regions
while bringing the whole kingdom with him.
Each time he can give the whole revelation,
each time he can give himself prodigally.

Father, my Son, Holy Spirit,
all of us who believe in you
give thanks for my Son's kingship,
in which the kingship of the Father and the Spirit
reveals itself visibly.
For his kingdom is the whole kingdom
of his Father and of the Spirit,
and he gives to each one of us
the whole heavenly truth of the Trinity.

Father, many will mock this King,
many will pretend to see nothing of this kingdom,
and yet you, Father,
in the midst of this mockery and blindness,

can communicate to all who seek you
something capable of strengthening their faith.
You will show them
that none of us would be capable of seeing
unless your grace granted him seeing eyes
that in our Son recognized the King,
eyes that in each of his words and in all his deeds
    perceived
your whole kingdom
and your whole truth.

Father, we all thank you,
and I am not alone in thanking you with those who
    believe,
your Son thanks you with us. *Amen.*

Mary on the Way of the Cross
Prayer to the Son

I CAN NO LONGER SPEAK to you, my Son,
as a mother speaks with her son.
I cannot get close enough.
I have only the anonymous place of the Christian,
the place you left free for me
when you chose me to be your Mother.
I wanted to become your Mother
and at the same time be a woman who believes in you.
And now we can only speak to each other as believers.

I see you carry the heavy Cross.
I cannot help you as your Mother,
I can only be near you with my faith.
And I adore you.
And I know that you, carrying the Cross,
are nevertheless also in heaven.
And I seek you in the presence of the Father
and adore you and offer you my bitter affliction,
and I pray you
that my pain may help you
to carry your Cross.

I also beg you
to grant that,
even when you will no longer be present,
my faith may be strengthened by you
and may be at the disposition of all those who belong
    to you and love you.
And let me be a Mother to them all.
The Mother of a Son killed by crucifixion,
the Mother of all Christians crucified with him,
the Mother of all suffering men
who believe in you, the Mother of all
who long for you and seek you.

Let me be a Mother of sorrows,
so that I may be near you in sorrow
as you are near all of us in sorrow. *Amen*.

Mary on the Way of the Cross
Prayer to the Father

M Y GOD, my Son's heaviest hour
is upon him.
I cannot help him.
And you will not help him,
because he is asking you to let him suffer.
And I ask you for help.
I ask you, accept his suffering.
Accept all of it.
I pray you, take my fear,
take my affliction, not away from me,
but to yourself,
so that my fear and my affliction
may be used according to the wishes of your
    Son.
I want no control over it.

My God, I am trying to give it to you,
and I know that all of us
who climb this hill
and see your Son suffer
would like to try to bear
what you give us to bear.
And we would like to bear it,
which is just what your Son,
who by your grace became my son,
wishes for all whom he loves.

For all those who do not have the faintest idea
    of his existence.
We know that our help is meager.
We women are here but have no strength.
You can give us the strength to bear.

Father, you entrusted your Son to me
by your Spirit.
And as I have given him back to you daily and hourly,
I give him back to you now once more,
knowing that his suffering is nothing other
than the expression of your grace,
the expression of your love.

It is hard to understand,
I do not understand it at all.
And yet I know
that I must give precisely this,
that you require it in this way.
And I ask you:
Take your Son out of my hands
—for he is my Son—
and take at one and the same time everything
I myself have given him
and which in this farewell hour
bears only the name of pain and grief.
Take it, dispose of it,
let my suffering become as heavy
as you will,
I know (your Son has taught me this)
that this is how I must pray in this hour. *Amen.*

Mary of Cleophas
at the Cross

Mary of Cleophas had no special relationship to the Lord up until this point. She had been induced to follow him more by the influence of others. She accepted the Lord's teaching like a woman of the people with a naïve faith, a naïve devotion and willingness. She would be ready to do the Lord favors, to mend his clothes and to cook for him, and even more, because through her own son she has some interest in his person. She understands only with effort the act of faith, the bond connecting her son to the Lord. Her faith is not strong and vigorous enough to bring her to a personal following on her own. She is a just woman who wants to do good, who would like to help even here, in the same way that she would give help to anyone else who needed it. Her faith remains somehow within the compass of Judaism. To her, Jesus is more the preacher of a new doctrine than the new doctrine in person.—Now she stands full of pity at the Cross. Jesus was good. He did not deserve this. And somewhere in the back of her mind she thinks: He did not deserve this because he was my son's master, and my son is, after all, right. But it is also all disciples and believers in general who did not deserve that their master should die so shamefully; she feels pity for them too. And she has pity on John, who she knows was a special friend of the Lord. And also for the sinful woman, because she can well imagine what it means for a sinful woman to become respectable, inwardly, emotionally, and intellectually, and then to fight against her surroundings, against gossip. And she feels pity for the Mother of Jesus, she guesses how terrible it must be for her to have to watch his torture and death as a mother. Staying near the Mother, she is also brought closer to the Son through her. The Mother opens to her the access to him. Through her pity on the Mother and through the Mother's demeanor, she begins to understand who the Son might be. Now her prayer comes to life. It begins to flow forth from the pity she feels for all who are present. She fulfills the commandment of love of neighbor. She has love for all the bystanders, who are becoming her neighbors. By this love of neighbor she comes to Mary, who immediately becomes the Mediatrix of her Son. And now she has attained surrender in faith and begins to pray according to it. This prayer at the Cross has given her an unbelievable new breadth:

F ATHER IN HEAVEN,
   I stand by with all who stand at the Cross.
I did not come as a mere spectator
but because I wanted to help.
I did not know what form my help was going to take.
I thought that maybe I could lend a hand here and
    there,
that maybe one of the women who had come along
    would get sick,
that maybe the Lord, in whom I do believe, would
    say something
that sounded like a will,
in which I, as a believer, would have had a share.
And now I see: I am here because you will it.
And you will it because your Son has decided
who is to be present at his dying hour.

And I am here like everyone else,
and yet in a particular way as if it were meant for
    me,
because your Son really does have a will,
which for me lies less in his words than in his death.
He wills that all of us who are here may have some
    idea
how great his sacrifice is.
And we all suffer together because he is suffering.
We no longer suffer because we are kindhearted
or eager to help, or because we have the compassion
of insignificant people,
but for the sole reason that he is suffering.
And we can no longer set a limit to
the suffering that fills us to the brim,
it is something new,
which reminds us of nothing we have experienced
    personally up until now.
It is a suffering imposed by God,
a suffering in which we recognize our own sin
and the sin of the whole world
at the moment when the Son is atoning for us all.

Father, give me the strength
to suffer to the end.
Father, allow me so
to suffer with your Son
that his suffering comprehends mine.
Not in order to add to his suffering,
but so that the suffering of those

for whom he suffers may also be included
in his sufferings—
not just their sin, but also their suffering.

Father, I had attempted
to keep the commandment of your Son
and to love men.
I had attempted to see in my neighbor
the neighbors of the Lord.
That is why my love
for the Mother of the Lord came so naturally.
But thanks to her and to her love,
I have come to a new love
for your Son.

Father, let this love come alive,
give it the form you wish,
let this suffering last
as long as your Son suffers;
and I know
that he suffers not only as far as his own death
but also so long as we sin.
I ask you, Father,
grant me, as a sign that you see
that I now understand the love of your Son in a new
    way,
to bear as much suffering as you wish.
I know that even
the greatest human suffering
is nothing compared to that of your Son.

After this is over, Father, when
they have buried your Son,
I will return to my own affairs
and will perform my small daily chores,
but I beg you,
do not let us grow cold in our love for you
and for your Son and his Mother.
Do not let us grow cold in love
for our neighbor;
rather,
since we have just realized
that your Son is truly God,
let our love be
an answer to his love. *Amen.*

Mary Magdalen at the Cross

It is more a cry than a prayer. From the moment the Lord had redeemed her with his absolution, she had lived an entirely new life: contrition and thanksgiving and no more sinning. She knew what she had been freed from. She learned by experience what absolution is. She kept the commandment to sin no more. She worshipped and adored the Lord. She lived in him. But her vision of the Lord was still closely bound to her former sin, her contrition and her thanksgiving had a very personal coloration.—Now she stands at the Cross, and the Lord can no longer hear her with human ears. She prays to him as if he were already in heaven. And she knows that her prayer is heard in heaven.

L ORD, YOU HAVE SET ME free
from my whole life of sin.
Until now I saw how great my sin was;
every day I would call this pardoned sin to mind,
remembering how you forgave me.
I hoped that, by this recollection,
and by my gratitude for it, and by the faith that
binds me to you, I could do something for you.

And now, Lord, you suffer unspeakably,
and I see that this unutterable pain
is your answer,
not only to my sin,
which you have forgiven me,
but to every sin of the world.
And now I ask you, Lord,
and it is my own request,
let me atone with you, bear the burden with you,
suffer with you for the sins of the whole world.

Until now I saw only my sin,
which you have forgiven me.
Now I see that your task is infinite,
because you are forgiving the sin of the whole world,
of all who are sinners, like I was,
and who resist you.

And I see
how this task is too much for
your human powers and how you are dying
in impotence and in the inability to go on
and in overwhelming suffering.

I ask, therefore: Let me have a share of it.
Remember that you anticipated your Cross for me,
remember how easily you pardoned me.
And only now do I see
how much it costs to pardon sins.
So let me pay the price for some sinner,
for more than one, if that is your will,
I do not need to know which.
But let me pay;
from now on let my own forgiven sin disappear
among these other sins,
and let me also understand
your work of reconciliation so well
that I offer you every penance you decide to give me
for a use that is unknown to me.
Perhaps I can lighten some part of your work of
    forgiveness,
perhaps I can help prepare some sinner's way to you.

Take every one of my days and make of it
a day of penance and contrition and also of gratitude.
Let me promise here under your Cross
that I will try
in the future to do only what
you can require of me according to this Cross. *Amen*.

IV

THOUGHTS ON PRAYER

1. When you have contemplated reality for a long time from God's point of view, there can be a danger that you start wanting to express everything in vague Christian formulas. It is as if you are flying high above the earth and you cannot expect others to be able to catch up effortlessly to your way of seeing and thinking. This is why in the midst of my prayer I have to maintain the freedom and openness to see men realistically, to meet their expectations; I must especially be on my guard against speaking of God with "unction". There is no question that you offer men your genuinely Christian help, but you do it without churning out a lot of pious platitudes. You try to be in God and at the same time to stay near to men. You have to become all things to all men; you have to keep your sense of humor and your wit. No one should get the impression that he has no way into this "higher world". Nobody should have the feeling that if you pray, your prayer puts you even farther out of reach. Remain natural! And when you have tried to help people with their concerns, then afterward you will bring these concerns before God in prayer.

(*Nachlassbände* 10, no. 2093, p. 51)[1]

---

[1] The *Nachlassbände* are the as yet untranslated posthumous works of Adrienne von Speyr. Hereafter the title will be abbreviated "NB".

2. Every active mission remains incomplete as such. It is not possible to do everything. Not least so that the mission can be rounded out through suffering. But contemplation also rounds it out: the time you absolutely must subtract from action. Much that could be done must remain undone—even in the case of a very busy parish priest—for the sake of prayer.

(NB 9, no. 1933, pp. 418f.)

3. How can you make people understand that they are supposed to grow into prayer?—It is just like with a foreign language: you teach the pupil word by word. The language of God and the saints. And all at once they speak this language fluently. But this is possible only when you teach them the rudiments very clearly. In an I–thou relationship. Then the pupil also hears how the teacher speaks the language with others, he listens and acquires fluency. The teacher can be God himself or the Mother of God or a priest. But it does not absolutely have to be a human being. God can open up heaven to a child.

(NB 9, no. 1945, p. 246)

4. An old monk (perhaps Anthony) appeared and said . . . that at a certain point in time he had begun really to dedicate himself to prayer, with the feeling that prayer was a pursuit that filled up one's

life. Before that, when he was still in the world, he was already reputed to be an experienced Christian, and many came to him seeking advice. But his new prayer seemed to bear no fruit. It seemed to be of no help at all in his dealings with men; even when he had taken their concerns and questions into prayer, he came out no more enlightened than before. He therefore asked himself whether it would not be better to return to the apostolate and to save prayer for eternity. But he realized that this was a temptation and saw that he was being led out into the desert . . . in order to seek, to pray, and to learn from God there. At first it did not go at all well in the desert: he had many more annoyances than in the world. Sometimes he was too cold, at other times too warm; sometimes he was hungry, then it would rain again; sometimes he would be able to pray well for a longer period, but then it would prove impossible again. And all at once he realized that he himself was the greatest annoyance. There lurked in him a self-love that made him seek desperately after any distraction, just to be freed from prayer. It is not that he had been insincere before that, just that he had not noticed it because no one had pointed it out to him. Then he began to do two things. First, to fast. Initially, a little, then more and more, never exaggeratedly. He sought a measure of food that was exactly suited to his prayer. And he ate very uniform fare, which he prepared himself. If he had varied the menu, the question of food would have occupied too much of his attention. Second, he practiced exterior prayer postures. The idea was that prayer had to become the predominant force in him, to take over all the space—to push *him* more and more against the wall. Things went increasingly better, and people started coming to him again. At first, no one knew where he was; later on, he gradually moved back into his own country, and people found him. And since he no longer stood in his own way when he prayed, he could also help other men. He grasped that previously he had caught prayer in himself and had thereby frustrated its fruit. At the end he dwelt in his "accessible desert" in great indifference. It was all the same to him whether anyone paid attention to him or not.

From the moment he cut his own self out, he received an understanding of God's Trinity. For the truth is, he said, that as long as in prayer man experiences his own personality, he cannot come to know the threefold personal being of God. As long as the ego lives, it stands in a sort of partnership vis-à-vis God, the two are somehow comparable, and God cannot then be more differentiated in relation to man than man is himself.

(NB 9, no. 1980, pp. 448f.)

5. It once actually seemed to me as if the whole world were on its way down to hell. Some switch is shifted the wrong way and all at once you realize

that you are moving down the wrong escalator. I
wanted at most to go to purgatory, and suddenly I
am on the way to hell. What is so ludicrous about
it is that, if I am gliding along the wrong belt, I
at least have to watch that I do not fall. I have to
keep up a dignified appearance. I cannot afford to go
bottom first into hell. . . . This image leads to the
question of prayer. The people who glide along like
that would first have to be tripped up by a grace of
prayer in order then to get back on their feet again
in one way or another. If they manage to keep up
their balancing act, it is hard to see any solution for
them. In some circumstances you try to pray people
toward God; but in this case you get the feeling that
you have to use the main weight of your prayer just
to knock them down in the first place. The expen-
diture of effort is much more massive, perhaps less
differentiated as well, when you think of the new
forms of lay orders, of women in the factories or
of the worker priests; they can actually throw them-
selves between the wheels with their prayer, so that
even if they get crushed the car does come to a stop,
or at least drives ahead more slowly.

(NB 10, no. 2045, pp. 15f.)

6. . . . You can pick up the thread of prayer from
anything. Even a joy or a sorrow that you have experienced and that helps you to know God better, or
a story that someone has told me. Or some aspect of

the creation. And you can let yourself be led onward by anything. By a beautiful landscape; by beauty and brightness in general. By a plan I have: God's plan for us and for the world. When the things of this world open up expansively toward God, you are no longer the reference point but the point of reception for God's gifts. In almost every contemplation there comes the moment when you are concentrated receptivity and at the same time already distributed beyond yourself. I experience something of God, but the fact that it is I who experience it is from the very outset irrelevant: all that counts is that something more of that experience of God in the world will have prevailed.

(NB 10, no. 2058, p. 25)

7. Although every knowledge in faith is accompanied by an admixture of mystery, this does not mean that knowledge must therefore give up; on the contrary, one who prays ought to hope to be initiated more deeply into the mystery with time.

But if God entrusts a mystery to him and partially unveils it, it will primarily be God's prerogative to lead to a greater clarity. The man who prays knows that God is omniscient. God sees not only him perfectly but also the neighbor for whom he must now pray. God can disclose to him a more complete picture of this other man if he deems it necessary; but it can also be the case that God's divine knowledge remains sealed like a protective cover of mystery about this fellow man. Hence, the man who prays must abide patiently in a sort of abstraction; everything is played out in an act of self-surrender and of acceptance by God. It would be indiscreet to call things by name; God leaves in the dark how he will utilize this prayer. But what is abstract for man is concrete in God and at any moment can, if God so wills, become concrete also for the one offering the prayer; it can come to represent something that he recognizes, that serves him as a directive for his future conduct.

When the man who prays makes a concrete offer to God, God abstracts and generalizes it in order to make it concrete again later in an entirely different way, yet as part of a mystery that remains in God. And it is with his face turned toward this mystery that the believer must pray. Or live. Or act. The mystery does not dispense the believer from a clear stance, from having to be focused on something. He must not inhabit a "higher sphere" that no longer has anything to do with everyday reality under the pretext that he participates in an abiding mystery. . . .

Whoever asserts that he is so entangled in the net of contemplation that he no longer has eyes for the world around him would be giving bad testimony to the quality of his prayer. And just as Teresa of Avila interrupts her ecstasy to prepare a meal, every member of the Church, priest or layman, must interrupt his contemplation for the sake of an act of love of neighbor that has been required of him.

One final point: even if a mystery must remain inviolable in prayer, nonetheless little concrete practical applications for the man praying (*aliquem fructum capere*) always spring from it. These can be immediately put into practice. You can pray for the sin of the world as a whole, can receive some certain knowledge concerning this sin—though the greatest mass of it remains veiled—but suddenly the pray-er will see that he is covered with this sin at a very concrete spot and that it is high time to cleanse this particular point. It is like a corollary resulting from the main conclusion.

(NB 10, no. 2221, pp. 206f.)

8. If you pray on earth, you know that your prayer will be conveyed to the right place. You can send up to God the most personal, most urgent matters clothed in prayer. You can throw this prayer into the treasury of the Church. It then disappears in a certain sense, it makes its way with sure aim to its destination, which does not mean that the burden of what you must bear has been lessened. You have commended it to God, but that does not always simply mean relief.

In heaven, there seems to be a sort of quick settlement of affairs. If you recommend anything at all, you do it just briefly, certain that you have been heard and understood. On the other hand, you are drawn very deeply into things that do not expressly call attention to their urgency but that are simply there and into which you are yourself invited: heavenly concerns, God's demands on the world: you have no choice but to join in. It is unclear to you how it will be when heaven has become a permanent home. . . .

(NB 10, no. 2225, pp. 212f.)

9. Just as you can plunge into good music, you can immerse yourself in prayer. Without effort, just like you dive into the water. And the true musician simply serves the music. He does not concentrate on his own imperfection—"If only my fingers were less stiff, if only I had practiced more beforehand." Without reflecting on perfect or imperfect, he simply sets to work, even improvises, without preening himself. I play Schubert, not myself. And as for my distinctive style, I let it disappear into the Schubert. It is not my intention to "put on a show for you". In prayer, no artificial disclosure for its own sake. That only narrows the horizons. Do not be unhappy because the proper conditions are lacking.

(NB 10, no. 2094, pp. 51f.)

10. One is often interrupted in prayer on account of an external factor: you are disturbed, you have to

finish some work, or you are too tired. Then you
enter a self-contained world of deliberations, resolu-
tions, and expectations. And suddenly you remember that you are permitted to pray, and for a moment
everything else disappears. Prayer streams into you,
from all sides, as perfect refreshment for the spirit,
without your needing to see or to think anything in
particular or even to have a definite prayer theme. It
is simply God's world that breaks into man's world
and that makes you feel that you are a man and have
a body and senses and are and mean something that
can live in God's love and now experiences being
plunged into the world. Little by little something
emerges clearly, or else you pray with your heart
or lips with a definite intention, or else you hear
something, or you discover a new prayer or recite
an age-old one . . . and you see that the world in
which you lived before and that seemed so very
distant from anything divine was not really so far
beyond the pale. It could indeed appear for a few
instants as if it were cut off from contact with God.
But then the grace of this bath of prayer is so vast
that you know you may ask, adore, rest, that, in a
certain sense, you may do anything, inserted into the
reality that is offered you. And this reality goes beyond everything that could be expected or sought. It
is an unheard-of happiness that surpasses every hope
and has no room for anything but bliss.

(NB 10, no. 2166, p. 123)

11. . . . There are not enough saints. If God the Father, the Son, and the Holy Spirit created more worshippers who were truly surrendered to the tri-une mystery, some astounding things would be bound to happen. We would see the works of love of God accomplished on earth. But we do not al-low ourselves to be inflamed, we are not disposed, nor do we grasp that we do not have to trust our-selves to do it but God alone. When we are even in the least degree caught up and begin to understand something, it is solely through God's grace. And fi-nally there is the odd fact that God nonetheless gives us in his grace the fundamental Yes, that he gives us in faith and baptism a share in his eternal Yes, and that it is an essential characteristic of his courtesy to look upon this Yes of ours (which is his gift) when-ever he makes us an additional gift.

(NB 10, no. 2295, p. 295)

12. . . . Man cannot pray expressly without ceasing. But he can remain in an attitude of prayer. He can feel in himself the longing for eternity to such a de-gree that he perceives signs of eternity in all elaps-ing time; he has a certainty that he is bounded by eternity on every side. He cannot force God's eter-nal duration down to him. Nor can he tear holes in time himself. But the longing is there, and, when it is authentic, it comes from God and is not without a demand on man; God constrains him to live in the

eternal. And the principal characteristic of eternity is that it is "ever now". To pray now, to answer now, to follow God's call now. Heedless of whatever else is going on.

(NB 10, no. 2264, p. 255)

13. The experience that the whole of daily life—being, talking, and acting—pertains to prayer. Just as the Lord conceived everything he did as part of his conversation with the Father. In this way he inaugurated for us a new manner of praying. It goes without saying that this prayer cannot remain the only kind: one must set apart alongside it time for quiet prayer and meditation. But the point is that both, express prayer and lived prayer, form together the whole of prayer. If, therefore, someone ceases to pray and contemplate, his conversation with his fellow man also falls out of the compass of his prayer.

And it is no accident that the inflexible framework of the Church is ever present. There are prescriptions and decrees and all sorts of misunderstandings. The Church has a side whose friction serves as a spur to do more, to attempt new things. . . . When the outward difficulties presented by the Church are absent, my ego, with its personal difficulties, moves to the center, and everything contracts. Within the framework of the Church, however, I am constrained constantly to explain my position with respect to others, and the explanation need not be a personal one at all. At some point, which cannot be fixed, one is thrust into the living relationship between the Lord and the Church. . . .

(NB 10, no. 2330, pp. 327f.)

14. Waves come and go, no one can pin them down, they can never be calculated beforehand. If one attempts to follow the line of approaching waves backward, the eye soon fails and must give up. The ocean as an image of infinity, of eternity, the wave as the moment that comes and passes away and yet returns again and again, demanding something. One's mission comes from the eternal God imbued with eternity and resolves itself into moment-long, quick decisions and responses. At the shore one has the impression of being seized by an eternal event, and, if one is overcome by the fear of having missed a wave, a decision due at some particular moment, one is reassured by the fact that ever-new waves are coming and new responses are being demanded— so quickly that the new wave has already arrived before the last one has spread itself out over the sand and receded. The little wave is like action, and the vast ocean is like contemplation. The two are a unity; this unity is God, but it is shown to man over and over again in the wave. He is to act, but he cannot act except out of contemplation, he cannot make his decision except within God's great deci-

sion. And this also gives him a feeling of security: the wave, which in receding is always borne in the sea's protection, water in water, without having to maintain its personal countenance. In this way the many acts of those who belong to God are hidden safely in his all-embracing act and have in it their stability and their abode. The movement is constantly beginning anew: each wave receives its own contour, and each one loses it again and is itself lost in the whole. It remains present in the omnipresence, contained in the vast freedom of the waters, at home in the sea from which it came forth and was sent. Something similar is true in prayer. For a moment it has visage and form, that of petition or of adoration, say. But whatever it may have been, it returns into the whole. The individual prays only because countless men pray, will pray, and have prayed, because God does not grow weary of providing strength for prayer, of filling men's prayers with content and of granting even the most trivial request, so long as it comes from authentic faith. He receives it gladly and makes use of it in heaven, as if precisely this minuscule contribution completed the sum he was awaiting. One would think that the ocean is completely full only when this wave also returns to it. The sea has, as it were, lent it out to the shore, but its belonging to the origin continues. Thus, the contemplation of the ocean is an encouragement to prayer but also to gratitude. It is good to know oneself and one's prayer to be sheltered safely, good to know about infinite unity and to feel through all this God's love and to be able to return to it again and again.

(NB 10, no. 2229, pp. 217f.)

ON THIS EDITION

For Adrienne von Speyr, prayer does not begin at the usual starting point. One enters with her into a prayer that is already taking place and has been in full swing from all eternity—the trinitarian conversation of God with God, which is the primordial archetype of all prayer. This conversation is from its eternal origin already opened and offered to creation, which, in communion with the saints and, in particular, the Mother of the Lord, is permitted to participate in it in fact.

This small volume contains in somewhat looser form the prayers already published in 1968 by Hans Urs von Balthasar.

They include "prayers of the earth", which rise up into the opened heaven and with child-like naturalness carry everything with them: the new morning, the night, one's fellow man as he works, sorrows, and turns away from God, everything one has and does not have, even one's wickedness.

And there are "prayers of heaven", which "it would be more precise to characterize as prayers of the Church on earth as they sound before God's throne", since "there is just one Church on earth and in heaven." This is to pray the prayers we have received from heaven through the Apocalypse and which in all truth convey to us the experience of a "world of prayer" in which everyone and everything has long had and now finds its predestined place.

The (hitherto unpublished) "Marian prayers", which are so striking on account of their concreteness and naturalness, are added here. Five of them are prayers of the Mother of the Lord—rarely has her humanity in the midst of her singular election been taken so seriously—and one each is spoken under the Cross by Mary of Cleophas and Mary Magdalen.

A few texts of Adrienne on prayer conclude this little volume and may be considered her own objective and at the same time committed commentary on it. How gladly would she have handed on this torch of prayer already during her lifetime.

FEAST OF OUR LADY OF MT. CARMEL 1992